T0317115

HEATH ROBINSON'S
SECOND
WORLD WAR

HEATH ROBINSON'S
SECOND WORLD WAR

HEATH
ROBINSON

This edition first published in 2016 by the Bodleian Library
Broad Street
Oxford OX1 3BG

www.bodleianshop.co.uk

Original material reproduced from:
Heath Robinson at War, 1942
The Sketch, 1939-1942
The Aeroplane, 1941
Flight, 1941-1942
The Royal Air Force Journal, 31 October 1942

ISBN: 978 1 85124 443 0

Cover design by Dot Little
Designed and typeset in 12/17 Obelisque by Roderick Teasdale
Printed and bound in China by C&C Offset Printing Co. Ltd on 157gsm Chinese Huaxia sun matt art

British Library Catalogue in Publishing Data
A CIP record of this publication is available from the British Library

CONTENTS

Foreword   7

Heath Robinson at War   13

Cartoons from *The Sketch*   61

The War in the Air   147

The Duo-Mask
for Married Couples

Respectability

Absence of Mind

The Smoker's Gas Mask

Forgetfulness

ALL ABOUT GAS MASKS

FOREWORD

William Heath Robinson was a brilliant artist whose ambition was to be a landscape painter. However, he soon discovered that his landscapes would not earn him a living. He worked first as an illustrator and by the early 1900s was acknowledged as one of the leading illustrators of the age. A publisher's failure to pay him for a major project led him to try his hand at humorous art and he was soon being fêted as a unique talent in this field too. By 1914 he was balancing the two careers of illustrator and humorous artist. In his autobiography he wrote that:

> One day I might be illustrating Kipling's *A Song of the English* or a Shakespeare play and the next would find me at work explaining the Gentle Art of Catching something. It was always a mental effort to adapt myself to these changes, but with the elasticity of my early days, it was not too difficult.[1]

The onset of the First World War resulted in a sharp decline in the demand for fine illustrated volumes, but this was accompanied by an increased interest in Heath Robinson's unique style of humour. Over the next four years he applied his gentle brand of satire to both the enemy and friendly forces with telling effect in his weekly cartoons in *The Sketch* and more occasional work for a number of other periodicals. These drawings were collected at the time in a series of publications from Duckworth and are now available in *Heath Robinson's Great War.*

In the years following the First World War the demand for illustrated books had all but disappeared and he depended to a greater extent on his humorous work. Commissions from magazines such as *The Bystander, The Strand, Pearson's* and *The Humorist* occupied the majority of his time. However, his wartime popularity had led to requests for his services for advertising. During the war he had found time to make drawings to promote the virtues of 'Chairman' tobacco and to show how Johnnie Walker whiskey is made. Throughout the inter-war years he was regularly employed by companies keen to have their product associated with the positive feelings that his humorous drawings engendered.

In the summer of 1922 the publisher George Newnes launched a new magazine called *The Humorist,* edited by Reeves Shaw, which was aimed at the expanding middle classes and intended to rival *Punch* with its light-hearted mix of drawings and prose. The publisher was keen to recruit Heath Robinson as a contributor to the magazine. At the time he was making a weekly drawing for *The Bystander* and contributing to several other magazines, so only managed to supply a few cartoons, but in 1928 he ceased work for *The Bystander* and his contributions to *The Humorist* became more regular.

By the time of the Munich crisis in September 1938, everyone in Britain had been issued with a gas mask. Heath Robinson's first drawing related to the Second World War was published in *The Humorist* in November with the title 'All About Gas Masks'. It was followed in May 1939 by 'The sort of thing you are supposed not to do with your Air-raid shelter' and 'More Reserved Occupations'. In September 1939 readers were shown 'How to Black Out' (while reading in bed, in the dining room and while bathing baby) and 'Unobtrusive Ways of Carrying Your Gas-mask'. Heath Robinson's last cartoon for *The Humorist* was published at the end of November 1939 and reflected the 'Phoney War', showing 'Christmas Games for Our Soldiers at the Front'.

In September 1939 *The Sketch* published the first of a weekly series of drawings that showed how 'Our Special Artist, Mr W. Heath Robinson' imagined things to be, first on the Siegfried line and then with the British Army, a selection of which are reproduced in this book. They showed a 'cleverly camouflaged all-ways gun' and 'washing day' and 'bath night during an air raid' on the Siegfried line. Scenes with the British Army showed 'putting down a leaflet barrage before an infantry attack' and a 'magnetic trench clearer'. The editorial accompanying the former title describes it as:

> … a superb example of the nearly-workable mechanical contrivances associated with his name.

Five of the drawings published during October and November were reproduced in the American magazine *Life*. The accompanying text observed that:

> Robinson's ability to laugh off war and to take indiscriminate pokes at friend and foe alike is an English trait. German war cartoons are bloodthirsty in their hatred of Britain. French war cartoons are feline in the ridicule they heap upon the Nazis. Somehow, however, English humorists still manage to keep an extra smile on tap for self-ridicule.[2]

It was very rare for Heath Robinson to depict real people in his drawings, but on 27th December 1939 the first of a series of 13 drawings appeared in which he showed the imagined exploits of a Winston Churchill 'super hero' as he attempts to win the war singlehanded. The series was titled 'The Ubiquitous Winston' and refers to him as 'the First Lord of the Admiralty', his post prior to Chamberlain's resignation. During the First World War Heath Robinson had shown the Germans attempting to infect our Tommies with 'flu germs. This time the First Lord and his Gang plot to inject 'flu germs into Field-Marshal Goering. As with the 'Saintly Hun' drawings in the First World War, Heath Robinson is at his most drily ironic, reversing the usual depiction of the German character as the Nazis are described as 'innocent and honourable creatures' against whom Churchill wages a 'campaign of frightfulness'.

Christmas Games for our Soldiers at the Front

To a far greater extent than in the previous conflict, the Second World War was fought on the home front. On 8th January 1940 bacon, butter and sugar were rationed and other commodities soon followed. Heath Robinson responded by inventing a series of 'rational gadgets for your coupons'. Nine drawings on this theme appeared during the spring of 1940 with a further two the following year. The focus on the home front continued with one of Heath Robinson's most ingenious concepts, the 'Sixth Column'. This was a well-organized group of patriotic civilians whose aim is to frustrate the plans of enemy agents and sympathisers, collectively known as 'Fifth Columnists'. The doughty citizens dislodge an enemy machine gun post from the dome of St. Paul's Cathedral, provide a warm welcome for enemy parachutists and prevent railway signals and even Big Ben from being tampered with.

The success of German forces invading France and Belgium in the early months of 1940 brought the prospect of invasion to Britain's shores and by May preparations for resistance were underway. That summer Heath Robinson published a series of drawings showing 'How to make it Hard for the Invader' with schemes such as 'the melted butter tank-stopper' or 'pinching the screwdriver to delay the assembling of air-borne tank parts'. Rotating signposts to confuse the enemy was offered as an alternative to their removal. During the latter part of the year the emphasis switched to 'Making it Hard for the Raiders', ways of frustrating enemy aircraft and for clearing up after an air raid.

As well as providing a weekly drawing for *The Sketch*, Heath Robinson was commissioned to illustrate *Mein Rant* a verse parody by R.F. Patterson of Adolf Hitler's *Mein Kampf*. More importantly, he teamed up with his Highgate neighbour Cecil Hunt to write another in his series of 'How to…' books. During the 1930s Heath Robinson's reputation as 'the gadget king' had been cemented by the series of four books that he had written with K.R.G. Browne that started with *How to Live in a Flat*. There were three further titles dealing with motoring, gardening and fatherhood, and the series was only ended by the premature death of Browne. Cecil Hunt had already published a number of humorous books and had been fiction editor of the *Daily Mail* and the *Evening News* and was a regular broadcaster. Together they produced *How to Make the Best of Things*, a book of advice on coping with the blitz, shortages, the black-out, the need for economy and showing how to manage holidays and recreations in wartime.

From the end of 1940 there are occasional drawings featuring Italian forces, who provided a much less dreadful subject than the Nazis. They include 'Mussolini's secret weapon disclosed – New back-action guns and equipment to enable retreats to be fiercely executed'. More frequent are references to the use of camouflage which seems to provide scope for endless humour. They range from 'A plan for the protection of our statue population' to a wonderful drawing showing how the Colonel's breakfast can be delivered safely to his table while enemy aircraft fly overhead. In 'Carrying on at Wimbledon' even the ball is camouflaged as a bird. These subjects are interspersed with the more familiar themes of countering a German invasion and surviving the blitz. One of the most ingenious ideas shows how a rotating anti-aircraft gun emplacement might be mounted on The Monument.

In 1941 Heath Robinson received his last advertising commission, to make a series of drawings for a company called High Duty Alloys that manufactured components for aircraft. The series of eight drawings titled 'The War in the Air' took phrases of RAF jargon or slang and illustrated each with an appropriate drawing in his inimitable style. They were published in *Flight* and *Aeroplane* magazines between September 1941 and June 1942. Prints of the first four, suitable for framing, were available on request. That year also saw the publication of his second collaboration with Cecil Hunt. This was *How to Build a New World* which, while gently satirising town planning, also reflected the hopes and aspirations of the British people in the second year of the war.

In October 1942 Methuen published a collection of Heath Robinson's cartoons from *The Sketch* under the title *Heath Robinson at War*. The 48-page booklet was bound in blue card wrappers and had a bright dustwrapper in yellow and black. As for the collections made during the previous conflict, the 22 full-page drawings that had first appeared in the magazine were complemented by a number of line drawings specially drawn for the book. On the half-title he drew a portrait of himself as the imagined war artist arriving in theatre and his expression shows what he thought of this dreadful war.

The last of Heath Robinson's war cartoons appeared on 25th March 1942. A break of two months, possibly indicating a period of ill health, elapsed before he reappeared with a final series of 11 drawings satirising the popular wartime radio programme *The Brains Trust* in which a panel of experts answered questions sent in by listeners. In *The Sketch* Heath Robinson suggested answers to such questions as 'Do Fish Sleep?' and 'How is the Ship's Anchor Weighed'.

His third wartime collaboration with Cecil Hunt was *How to Run a Communal Home* (1943) which explored a possible solution to the anticipated post-war housing shortage. It inspired some of his most pleasing drawings of the period. Sadly, he did not survive to see the end of the conflict and the building of the new and better world he had foreseen. He fell ill in August 1944, had an exploratory operation and was pronounced fit for a major operation, but on the 13th September 1944, before this took place, he died from heart failure.

Geoffrey Beare
The William Heath Robinson Trust

[1] *My Line of Life*, p119.
[2] *Life*, 25 Dec 1939, Vol 7, No 26, pp4-6.

Invasion Practice in Enemy Occupied Countries

HEATH ROBINSON AT WAR

The War Artist Arrives

Realistic Invasion Exercises

INTRODUCTION

HOW can I help the war effort? This is a question that has perplexed me since the outbreak of hostilities. It is a question that has caused me more depression, heartaches, headaches, neuralgia and mental indigestion than all of the restrictions necessarily inflicted upon us in these anxious days. I feel that it is now time to do something about it, if I am to make my influence felt in the successful prosecution of the war.

The first question that arises is, how can my rather unique talents be most profitably employed? In which of the many services shall I enrol myself? For the purposes of this note, these may be classified into two main fronts: firstly, the Fighting or Combatant Front, and secondly, the Home Front. For reasons into which I will not enter here, my services are not required in the former, while the latter does not offer many opportunities for the exercise of any talents I may possess other than those that may be displayed in carrying out my duties as a responsible and respectable citizen, willing, if not eager, to pay Income Tax when humanly possible. I have done my best to fulfil these obligations, but this is not enough. The monotony of a life thus circumstanced is bearable, but what is not to be borne is the sense of opportunities slipping past and a feeling of frustration. Instead of an intellectual organ bubbling over with ideas and bursting with enthusiasm, my brain must appear to my fellow-countrymen as an empty shell, a mere vacuum – in fact, a square hole in a round peg with nothing in it for any evidence he has to the contrary.

To meet the difficulties of this peculiar situation, and after consultation with many heads of departments, I have decided to form a front of my own, to be called the Heath Robinson Front to distinguish it from all the other Fronts on the earth, in the sea and in the air. It is proposed that this new front shall not function in any departmental manner. It will combine in one stupendous effort the activities of the already established fronts, to whose success it will contribute materially.

I feel that I cannot provide better propaganda for this new movement than will be found in this little brochure. It will, I hope, sufficiently explain the attitude to the war we intend to maintain. It will demonstrate the uniqueness of our approach to the difficulties confronting us. At the same time it will introduce many new and unheard of instruments of warfare. These may or may not be adopted by the War Office.

It would be an over-statement to say that I had been encouraged by the reception of my suggestions by that august body. This, I am convinced, is not due to their want of appreciation, and I would be the last to suggest that their decisions had been influenced in the smallest degree by a slight feeling of jealousy, which after all would not have been unnatural.

Be that as it may, I am sure that I can safely leave my reputation as a promoter of my country's welfare in the hands of those who study this book, and who, remembering my invaluable contribution to the successful conclusion of the last war, will be confident of my help in this.

W.H.R.

Come To The Cook-House Door

The Aerobumper

HUN CUNNING
Stormtrooper Armed
with Bow and Arrow
Disguised as Rifle

A Cleverly Thought Out Scheme for Smashing Enemy Tanks
on the Dover Road

An Opportunity Not to be Missed

The H. & C. Tank for Bath Nights

Deceiving the Invader as to the State of the Tide

The Tripedal Ski Gun

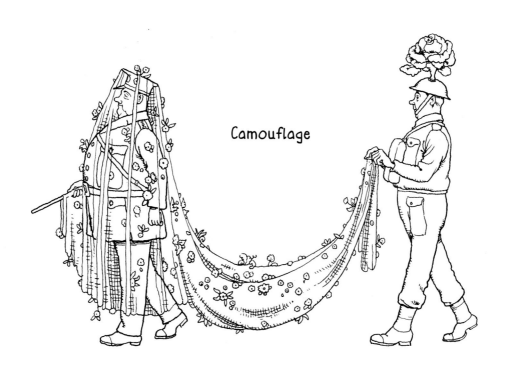

Camouflage

HITLER'S NEW SECRET WEAPON
The Aero-Tank Invented for Invasion Purposes

Loot

Holding up Enemy Advance Across Bridge Over
the Upper Reaches of the River Lea

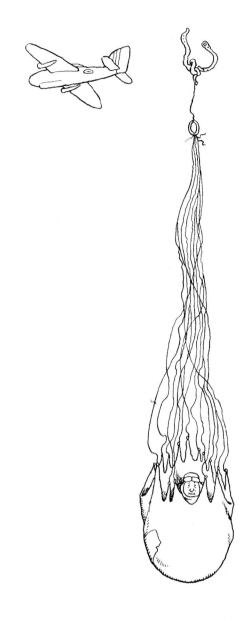

The Wrong Way to Come Down
in a Parachute

Here They Come! Disguised Parachutists Receive a Warm Welcome

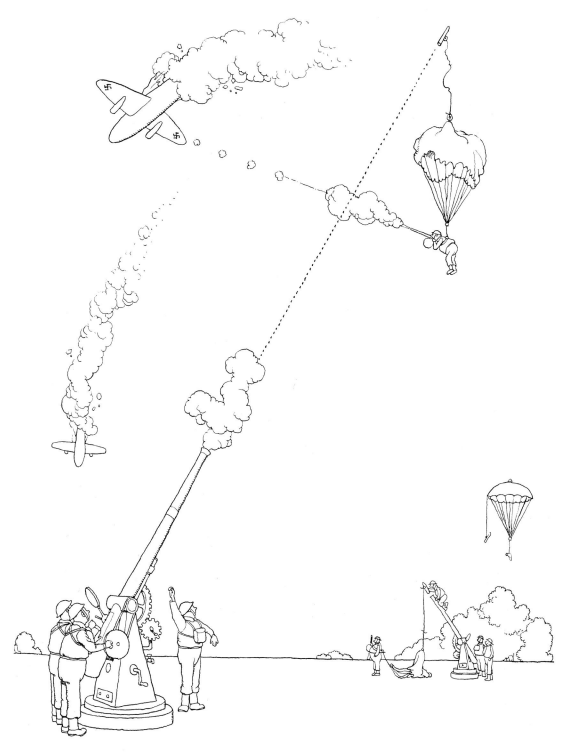

How to go up in a Parachute

Safe Practice for Paratroops

Guerrilla Tactics

Farmyard Camouflage

CAMOUFLAGE V. CAMOUFLAGE
During Invasion Practice on the East Coast

Jungle Camouflage

Interesting Experiments in Camouflage during
Manoeuvres on Salisbury Plain

Desert Panic

The Mirage in the Desert

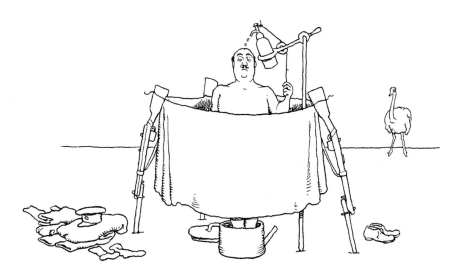

A Desert Shower Bath

THE OASIS TRAP
Capturing a Thirsty Detachment of Blackshirts in the Desert

The Colonel's H. & C. Tank

A New Tank with Piano Adjustment for Camp Concerts

Camouflaging the Colonel's Breakfast

Economy in the Making of Brides' Cakes

Economy in the Making of Anchovy Sauce

DESERT WARFARE
The Macaroni Mine

Learning to Sandbathe for when Water is Scarce

Training a Young Hun for Desert Warfare

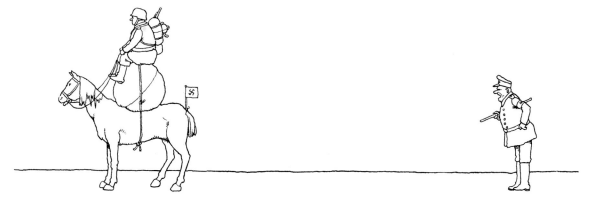

Lessons in Camel Riding

The Secret of How our Parachute Troops Get Back Again
is at Last Disclosed

Equitable Distribution of Loot

Upsetting the Enemy's Range-Finding by Confusing his Sense of Distance

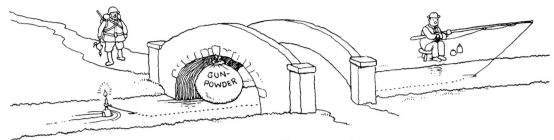

Primitive Guerrilla Strategy

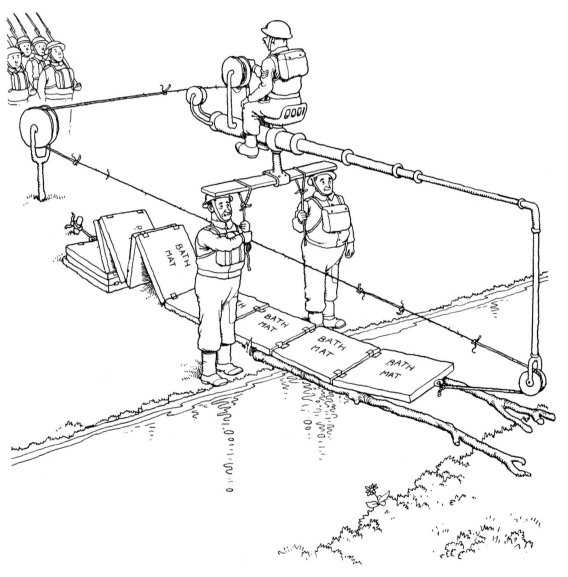

The Cork Mat Method of Crossing Streams

Cooling Buoys Lowering the Temperature of the Gulf Stream to Chill
the Ardour of our Enemy in the Battle of the Atlantic

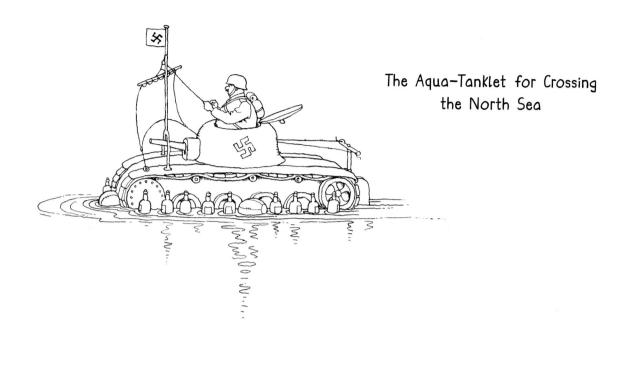

The Aqua-Tanklet for Crossing
the North Sea

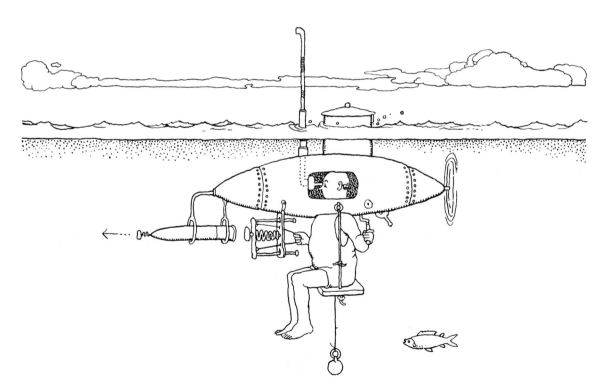

The One Man Submarine

Clever Ruse by British Submarine to Destroy Enemy Raider

Camouflaged Mines Luring the Invaders to Destruction

Heroic Attempt to Convoy Light Refreshments to Italian Troops Through a Minefield in the Mediterranean — Escorted by Fighter Aircraft

Legitimate Method of Stretching
the Tripe Ration

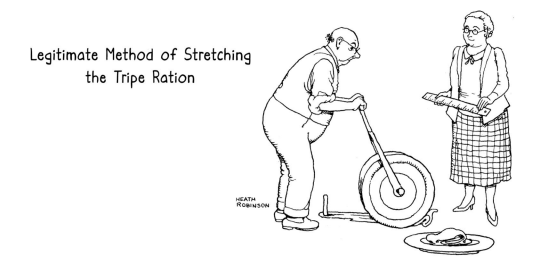

A Forgotten Guest

Spotting for Small Commercial Premises

'Tis an Ill
Wind that —

The Self-Registering
Belt Tight'ner

Protection for Statuary and Other Prominent Features
in London Squares During Air Raids

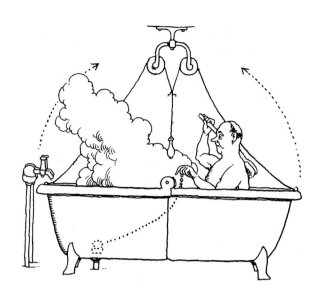

The A.R.P. Bath

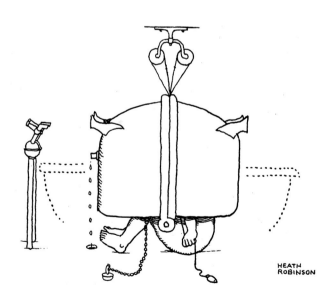

HEATH
ROBINSON

The Ever-Ready Bedside Bomb Extinguisher for Extinguishing Incendiary Bombs in the Bedroom Without Leaving Your Bed

Shrapnel Trousers for Air Raid Wardens

The Ball and Socket Anti-Aircraft Gun

On the Spot with the New Top Flat Rescue Apparatus — Coming to the
Assistance of Two Musicians in a Perilous Situation

Just in Time

A.R.P.

How to Remind Yourself not
to Forget Your Respirator

From Bedroom to Shelter in One Movement

A Comfortable Landing

CARTOONS FROM
THE SKETCH

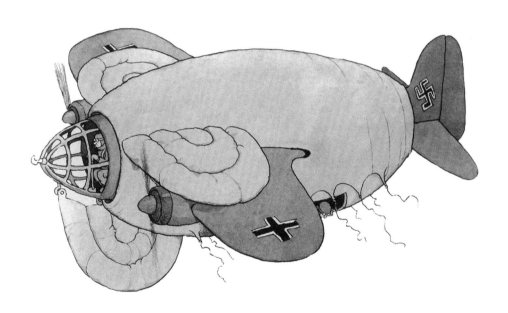

OUR SPECIAL ARTIST IN THE SIEGFRIED LINE
A Cleverly Camouflaged All-Ways Gun

OUR SPECIAL ARTIST IN THE SIEGFRIED LINE
Washing Day

OUR SPECIAL ARTIST IN THE SIEGFRIED LINE
Bath Night During an Air Raid

OUR SPECIAL ARTIST IN THE SIEGFRIED LINE
A Squadron of our New Hedge-Hoppers in Action

OUR SPECIAL ARTIST IN THE SIEGFRIED LINE
Disguised Anti-Aircraft Activities

OUR SPECIAL ARTIST WITH THE BRITISH ARMY
Putting Down a Leaflet Barrage Before an Infantry Attack

OUR SPECIAL ARTIST WITH THE BRITISH ARMY
The Relay System for Conveying Light Refreshment to Advanced Posts

OUR SPECIAL ARTIST WITH THE BRITISH ARMY
The Magnetic Trench-Clearer

OUR SPECIAL ARTIST WITH THE BRITISH ARMY
Armoured Pill-Box Crackers in Action

OUR SPECIAL ARTIST WITH THE BRITISH ARMY
The Hit-or-Missler Gun, for Firing in All Directions at One Time

OUR SPECIAL ARTIST WITH THE BRITISH ARMY
Our New Trench-Sealers Operating on Enemy Trenches in the Siegfried Zone

OUR SPECIAL ARTIST WITH THE BRITISH ARMY
How to Cross the Rhine Without Getting Wet

OUR SPECIAL ARTIST WITH THE BRITISH ARMY
'Netting' Tanks for Dealing with a Threatened Menace on the Western Front

THE UBIQUITOUS WINSTON
Disguised as a Coal Merchant, The First Lord Plots a Dastardly
Outrage Against Hitler

THE UBIQUITOUS WINSTON
Disguised as a German U-Boat, the First Lord Torpedos Ducks in the Round Pond to Give the Nazis a Bad Name

THE UBIQUITOUS WINSTON
Mr Churchill Makes Yet Another Attempt to Blacken the Fair Name of the
Nazis by Electrocuting a Welsh Rabbit on the Foothills of Snowdon

THE UBIQUITOUS WINSTON

Mr Churchill Sows Magnetic Mines on the Thames, so as to Lay Yet
Another Unsupporting Belligerent Act at the Door of the Innocent Nazis

THE UBIQUITOUS WINSTON
A Cowardly Attempt to Kidnap Lord Haw-Haw

THE UBIQUITOUS WINSTON
An Infamous Attempt by the First Lord to Steal the Bait
of a Fisherman in the North Sea

THE UBIQUITOUS WINSTON
Disguised as a Neutral, the First Lord Launches Another
Outrage on the German Navy

THE UBIQUITOUS WINSTON
Contemptible Plot by the First Lord and his Gang to
Inject 'Flu' Germs into Field-Marshal Goering

THE UBIQUITOUS WINSTON
The First Lord of the Admiralty in his
Specially Designed Mine-Sweeper

THE UBIQUITOUS WINSTON
Inhuman Conspiracy, Worked Out by the First Lord of the Admiralty,
to Kidnap Goering's Baby

THE UBIQUITOUS WINSTON
Device Invented by the First Lord for Deceiving Enemy Submarines
when Attacking a Convoy

THE UBIQUITOUS WINSTON
New Ideas for Arming our Merchantmen with Depth-Charges
and Other Anti-Submarine Devices

THE UBIQUITOUS WINSTON
The First Lord's Special Cloud–Dispeller Discovering
a Heinkel Bomber Hidden in a Cloud

RATIONAL GADGETS FOR YOUR COUPON
The Sunday's Joint

RATIONAL GADGETS FOR YOUR COUPON
Rationing Butter by Weight of Customer

RATIONAL GADGETS FOR YOUR COUPON
When Tea, as well as Sugar, is Rationed

RATIONAL GADGETS FOR YOUR COUPON
If Eggs are Ever Controlled: The Automatic Rationer

RATIONAL GADGETS FOR YOUR COUPON
A Communal Smoke at the Club Should Tobacco be Controlled

RATIONAL GADGETS FOR YOUR COUPON
Pushing Up Your Own Spirit: Petrol According to Horse-Power

RATIONAL GADGETS FOR YOUR COUPON
If Trouserings were Rationed: How to Draw Lots for a New Pair of Bags

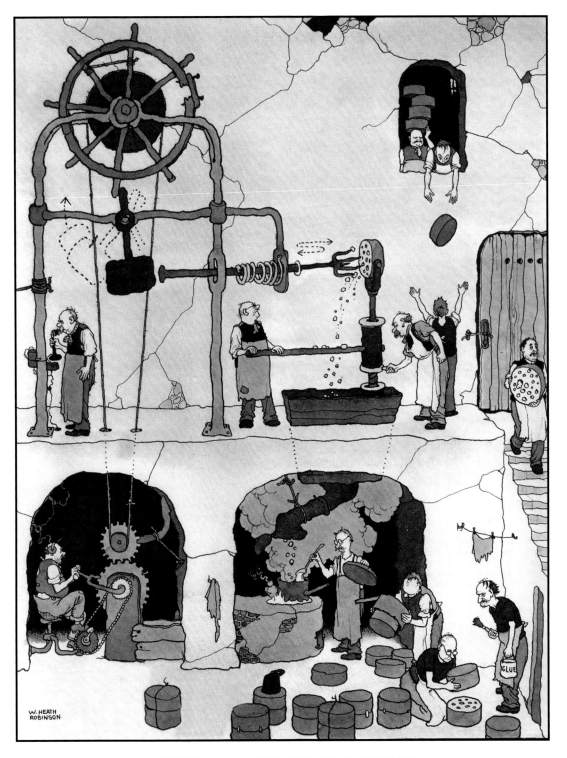

RATIONAL GADGETS FOR YOUR COUPON
Doubling Gloucester Cheeses by the Gruyère Method

RATIONAL GADGETS FOR YOUR COUPON
Stretching Spaghetti by the New Magnetic Method

BRITISH SECRET WEAPONS TO SURPRISE THE BOCHE
The Jumping Tank

BRITISH SECRET WEAPONS TO SURPRISE THE BOCHE
The Jerry Scarer. A New Mortar

BRITISH SECRET WEAPONS TO SURPRISE THE BOCHE
The Banana–Skin Tank–Skidder

SIXTH COLUMN STRATEGY
Sixth Columnists Frustrating a Vain Attempt by the Fifth
to Poison Pigeons in Trafalgar Square

SIXTH COLUMN STRATEGY
Frustrating a Dastardly Attempt by the Fifth Columnists
to Tamper with a Railway Signal

SIXTH COLUMN STRATEGY
Frustrating an Attempt to Disorganize London by Altering 'Big Ben's' Time

SIXTH COLUMN STRATEGY
Stout Patriots Dislodge an Enemy Machine-Gun Post
from the Dome of St. Paul's

HOW TO MAKE IT HARD FOR THE INVADER
The New Scissor Anti-Tank Trap Operating Near the Coast

HOW TO MAKE IT HARD FOR THE INVADER
An Anti-Tank Trap on the Brighton Road

HOW TO MAKE IT HARD FOR THE INVADER
Pinching the Screwdriver to Delay the Assembling of Air-Borne Tank-Parts

HOW TO MAKE IT HARD FOR THE INVADER
The Melted Butter Tank-Stopper Doing Its Stuff

HOW TO MAKE IT HARD FOR THE INVADER
The Stirrup-Pump Relay System of Signalling

HOW TO MAKE IT HARD FOR THE INVADER
Confusing the Enemy's Sense of Direction at Cross-Roads in a Rural Parish

HOW TO MAKE IT HARD FOR THE INVADER
Disguising the Depth of a Mill Stream to Form a Trap

HOW TO MAKE IT HARD FOR THE INVADER
An Adaptation of the Molotov 'Breadbasket' for Use in London Suburbs

HOW TO MAKE IT HARD FOR THE RAIDERS
The Multimovement Bomb-Catcher

HOW TO MAKE IT HARD FOR THE RAIDERS
A Brilliant Plan for the Deception of Dive-Bombers

HOW TO MAKE IT HARD FOR THE RAIDERS
The New Mobile Water-Gun for Quieter Anti-Aircraft Barrage

HOW TO MAKE IT HARD FOR THE RAIDERS
The Safe Way with Delayed-Action Bombs

HOW TO MAKE IT HARD FOR THE RAIDERS
A New Gadget for Blowing Out Parachute Flares

HOW TO MAKE IT HARD FOR THE RAIDERS
The 'Spotter's Friend' for Returning the Enemy's Fire

HOW TO MAKE IT HARD FOR THE RAIDERS
The Latest Machine for Dealing with Incendiary Bombs

HOW TO MAKE IT HARD FOR THE RAIDERS

Machinery for Discovering if a Delayed-Action Bomb is Alive

HOW TO SAVE LABOUR IN RAID CLEARANCE
The Shrapnel Collector

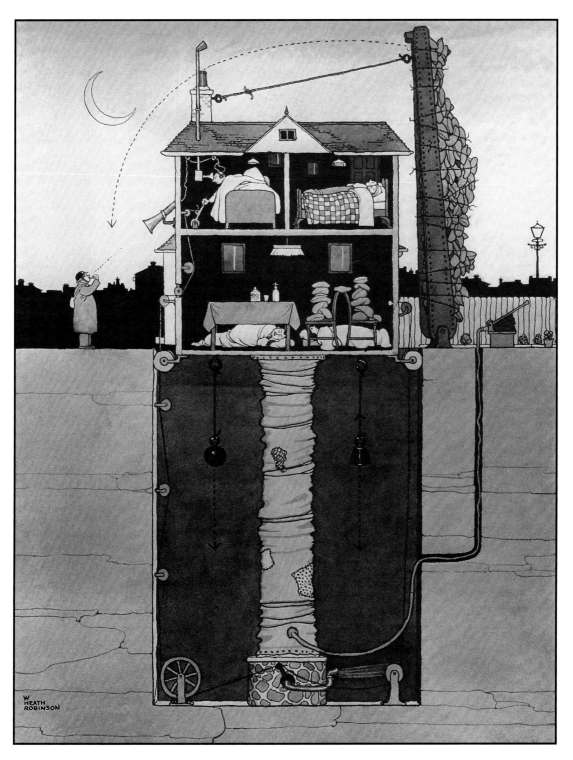

HOW TO GO TO GROUND WITHOUT GETTING UP!
The Disappearing Villa for Air-Raid Safety

MAKING SURE OF A HAPPY WARTIME CHRISTMAS
The Anti-Aircraft Spring Gun for Sending Presents to the Enemy

FIRE-WATCHING SIMPLIFIED
How to Know When There's an Incendiary in the Loft

Fire-Fighting on the Grand Scale

Mussolini's Secret Weapon Disclosed!

Patent Balloon Bursters Over London

Invasion Bells and the Fifth Column

How to Defend London

How to Meet Paratroop Invaders Halfway

Safety First! Camouflage in London Parks

Ever Ready on the East Coast

Carrying on at Wimbledon

The Whole Art of Anti-Dive-Bomber Camouflage

The New Magnetic Locator In Action

The Roof-Raising Defence to Defeat Dive-Bombers

How They Brought The 'Scharnhorst' from Brest to La Pallice

Foul Tactics!

The Enemy's New Caterpillar Triple Tanks for Invasion Purposes

Enemy Planes, Disguised as Barrage Balloons,
Landing Paratroops During an Invasion

A Way to Increase Your Greengage Jam Ration by
Installing New Machinery in an Old Jam Factory

Economical Method of Imparting the Pork Flavour to
Pork Sausages in a Wartime Factory

Some of our New Light Quisling Guns for Catching Quislings
Alive in Raids on Enemy Occupied Territory

Enemy Ice Mortars for Preventing Pursuit
When Crossing Frozen Rivers

A Battery of our Stale Ostrich-Egg Throwers for
Economising Ammunition in Desert Warfare

A New Method of Training Young German Ski-Troops to do the
Goose-Step on the Frozen Steppes of Russia

One Way Across the Channel! Nazi Troops are Rocketed from
Coastal Guns Operating from Enemy-Occupied Territory

THE WAR
IN
THE AIR

'THE WAR IN THE AIR' BY W·HEATH ROBINSON

Nº 1
BLIND FLYING
IS FLYING WHEN YOU CANT
EXACTLY SEE WHERE YOU
ARE GOING TO - THIS IS
HOW YOUNG PILOTS
ARE TRAINED TO DO IT

W. HEATH
ROBINSON

'THE WAR IN THE AIR' BY W HEATH ROBINSON

No. 4

THE CRATE

AN OLD FASHIONED BUT USEFUL TYPE OF MACHINE NOT YET ADAPTED TO WAR-TIME REQUIREMENTS

'THE WAR IN THE AIR' BY W·HEATH ROBINSON

Nº 5
THE CEILING
IS THE HIGHEST
POINT IN THE
STRATOSPHERE AT
WHICH THE CREW
CAN CARRY ON
AND THIS IS HOW
THEY KNOW WHEN
THEY GET THERE

'THE WAR IN THE AIR' BY W·HEATH ROBINSON

Nº 8
MANŒUVRABILITY
IS THE POWER TO
TURN ROUND QUICKLY
AND DODGE THE SNAGS
IN THE LINE OF FLIGHT

HEATH ROBINSON

Coquette

A Neat Apparatus for
Testing Your Own Gas Mask

Brighter Sausage Making in the
New R.A.F. Kitchens